Wisdom's Foresight

3rd Edition

FROM CATARACTS TO PANDEMIC VACCINES TO NEW HORIZONS

Preston Love, Jr.

©2022 Preston Love Jr.
All rights reserved. Except for brief excerpts for review purposes, no part of this book may be reproduced or used in any form without written permission from the publisher. The information in this book is from previously published articles and other written works and speeches by the author. Any product names and services known to be trademarks, registered trademarks, or service marks are property of their respective holders.

Preston Publishing
c/o Concierge Marketing Inc.
4822 South 133rd Street
Omaha, NE 68137
www.PrestonLoveJr.com

Paperback: 978-1-7345879-7-5

Library of Congress data on file with publisher.
Cover photo by Jason R. Fischer at Surreal Media Lab

Text design and layout by
Lisa Pelto, Concierge Marketing, Inc.
Vince Lindenmeyer, Ph.D., The LowCountry Group

4Urban logos and art by Shelby Adams, University of Northern Colorado

Parts of this book were originally published in the *Omaha World-Herald* Newspaper, and are reprinted in this collection with permission:

Love, Preston, Jr. "The pandemic of racism has endured and grown. It's time to listen." *Omaha World-Herald*, June 7, 2020

Love, Preston, Jr., "Understand North Omaha's past to chart the best course for the future." *Omaha World-Herald*, June 14, 2020

Love, Preston, Jr. "Real change for North Omaha will start with investments." *Omaha World-Herald*, June 21, 2020

10 9 8 7 6 5 4
Printed in the United States of America

Wisdom's Foresight

The continuation of *Economic Cataracts*

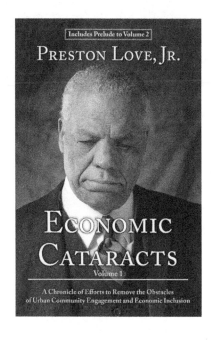

Free Labor, 1619-2019, 400 years

Dedicated to my loving wife, Martha Parker-Love.

Together we pray for all those suffering.

Contents

Introduction 1

What's Next Omaha? Recognizing The Issues 5

What's Next Omaha? Strategic Investment 9

Preamble: North Omaha's Bermuda Triangle 19

"Give Me Liberty…" 25

Blacks And The Vaccine 31

John Lewis: The First and the Last 37

Context, Compassion in the Poindexter Case 43

King's Dream Is Not Achieved as
Nebraska Carries Out Assaults on Democracy 49

The Horrible Cycle of Voter Suppression 55

Racism's Tug-Of-War with Democracy 61

Lessons From My Journey (A Call to Action) 67

Summer 2021 Is Time to Celebrate
Black Culture Once Again 73

"They Watched Us Pray" — Omaha Youth Visit Southern
Civil Rights Sites 77

Redistricting In Nebraska 83

2024: The Fall of the Empire?..89

Save Our Children..95

North Omaha Begins A New Chapter............................101

Your Bridge To History
By Portia Love & Preston Love Jr. 108

2019 Black Votes Matter Face-To-Face
With Black History Tour 110

An Octogenarian's Insights 125

North Omaha Legacy Tour 128

BVM "Face-To-Face With Black History"
Youth & Adult Tour..135

General Workshops, Speaking Events 137

| AN ESSAY COLLECTION |

Introduction

The greater discussion for this era, and for this generation, may be called the "Historical Moment" in the History of the United States; that this country finally attempted to face, discuss, and maybe, make major changes to the American structure of life and a time forced to confront the survival of democracy. That change will have been the recognition that systemic racism has, and does exist, and must ceremoniously, and structurally, be dismantled, for America to once and for all manifest its potential. The 13th, 14th, and 15th Amendments to the Constitution did not do it; the civil rights movement and its products—the 1964 Civil Rights Act, the 1965 Voting Rights Act, and the 1968 Fair Housing Act—did not do it. It was George Floyd, and his life and death that did it. I hope!!!

This book, *Wisdom's Foresight*, develops the most important elements during this historic time. These elements demand change and reform.

Those elements are:
- Policing: policy and practice
- Criminal Justice Reform: The entire range—from cradle to career—as it relates to the criminal justice system: intake, court systems, jail and prison systems, incarceration programs, privatization of prisons and more
- Mass incarceration: while part of the overall justice system, it requires its own focus
- Healthcare disparities: including healthcare delivery systems, mental and behavioral health disparities
- Educational achievement gaps and other disparities
- Urban community-based disinvestment: all of its parts, homeownership, entrepreneurship, development of wealth from poverty communities
- The assault on democracy

This book attempts to force conversation, learning, and dialog on these important elements dominating our country.

In this book, we first establish the baseline, which is the relationship between the two pandemics facing the country. They are the Covid-19 pandemic and systemic racism.

Second, we will develop and chronicle the evolution of one city's inner-city journey that became both poverty-stricken and an ugly showcase of disparities.

And thirdly, with that said, we will provide a recommended format, framework or blueprint for the disinvestment history of this inner city, and that is replicated throughout the country. The framework, or blueprint, is the fix—or said another way—it is what's next.

And last, we will present my voice of wisdom based on my experience, participation, and observation over a period of forty-plus years. That wisdom provides a unique foresight on multiple issues facing our country, our state and our locality.

Northeast corner of 24th & Lake, circa 1963.

―――― | AN ESSAY COLLECTION | ――――

What's Next Omaha?
Recognizing the Issues

A Noted African American scholar wrote "peculiar indifference to the magnitude of human suffering that racial disparities in health reflect," 1906.

We are currently suffering from not one, but two Pandemics. They are separate and distinct, but both contain a dramatic set of similarities, warnings, cries for help, and an urgent need for a "vaccine."

But first, let us reflect on a few historical reminders. I say a few, because there are far too many for me to cover in this short essay. As stated above, people of color, in particular African Americans, have suffered from social determinants as they relate to healthcare since the turn of the 19th century, as per the quote provided by W.E.B. Dubois. Let me be more specific. Several health determinants make Blacks and people of color more apt to be ill, less likely to receive treatment, and less likely to have access to health delivery systems.

- Poverty
- Race
- Nutrition, diets, and food security
- Job type
- Density of living
- Educational opportunities

These disparities have been voiced for centuries, from Dubois up to yesterday. However, the demand for recognition of the need for change, have been ignored, misunderstood, and denied.

So here comes Pandemic #1, the Coronavirus, and no surprise, as we collect and report the data, as it relates to race and other factors, the social determinants of health jump confirm. Blacks and people of color are diagnosed with the virus. They are dying at rates that are disproportionate with their numbers. For example, "minorities make up 27% of the Douglas County population and 73% of the positive cases."

And my point is that nobody has been listening. May I say that these social determinants can be pointed out throughout the full circle of life: healthcare, criminal justice, educational gaps, employment, community investments; all have been suffering from the same crisis, and nobody has been listening.

Pandemic #2 is systemic racism. Racism and its impact, has been in our country since 1619, when slaves were first brought to this continent. My race has endured slavery, indentured servitude, pervasive Jim Crowism, lynchings, redlining, bigotry, discrimination, the facade of democracy, inequality, and social injustice for over 15 centuries. Once again, we have a dramatic set of similarities to the virus warnings and an urgent need for a vaccine.

We thought we had a vaccine with some of the victories of the Civil Rights Movement, and progress sprinkled here and there. Still, the Pandemic of racism has endured and has grown despite our repeated calls for social justice. Not enough have been listening. Nationally we have had scores of documented and public senseless race killings, including recently George Floyd and of Black males by police and others. In my beloved hometown Omaha, we have had two lynchings, shootings by the police of a 15-year-old Black girl (Vivian Strong, 1969), and numerous other incidents leading up to the current tragic murder of James Scurlock. Our communities and its leaders have been suggesting, and in some cases demanding solutions, making suggestions and recommendations to address these racial determinants and disparities. The death of young Scurlock has, hopefully, opened up the eyes of the entire community of this systemic, racial problem, once and for all. Just like the Corona virus has opened up the eyes of this community to the aforementioned health and mental health disparities. Now we pray that our community will finally listen.

A vaccine for the Corona virus is in progress. The vaccine for racism is not. Our Omaha needs to listen, learn and respond to the people of color going forward.

Over the next month, we will continue with a weekly column dealing with specific suggested actions from the communities affected. We attempt to capture the dialogue and recommendations from the North Omaha Community, in some of the most important areas going forward, including police community relations, criminal justice reform, health and mental health disparities, strategic investments to impact our poverty-stricken community and jobs and wealth development within the community.

What's Next Omaha? *Listen.*

| AN ESSAY COLLECTION |

WHAT'S NEXT OMAHA? STRATEGIC INVESTMENT

As a native "Omahan" and years of accumulated wisdom as to the plight of my beloved race, I have a responsibility and a right to speak up during these tumultuous times. I do not have the right, however, to speak for my community. I am observing a tremendous surge of activism and conversation, from all segments of my community, from our elected officials, organizational leaders, to our lay leaders, and most importantly, our young leaders. Those conversations are intersectional, intergenerational, and healthy. The next generation is demanding to take the lead. I am impressed and take my place as an elder, not as a spokesman, but as an elder who is available for counsel. I, too, know and believe that Black Lives Matter. We jointly demand radical criminal justice change and new policing practices and policies, for we are in complete solidarity with specific recommendations emerging. I want to focus on another aspect of transformational change: strategic investment in our communities of color.

"North Omaha" had its beginning as a segregated, redlined, and intentionally economically deprived black section of the city. Blacks migrated north from the deep south to escape overt racism and to find work opportunities. Omaha's expansive meatpacking houses provided work to the ire and hate of whites who wanted all the jobs. We were villainized, neglected, even lynched, and murdered. We were under-employed and lacked financial resources. We were redlined, physically, financially, geographically, and psychologically. The Greater Omaha community adopted the narrative that blacks were inferior. As time passed, we were repeatedly reminded of our appointed station by banks, realtors, employers, public school systems, and teachers. "Stay in your place" was the term used by all. Yet, we had a secret weapon. We had strong influential clergy, a rich culture, and a determined resolve, segregated brilliant black educators, vibrant commerce, and stable family structures. The book *24th and Glory* (Chatelain, 2019), chronicles North Omaha's unbelievable and incredible reservoir of talent that emerged from the mid-20th century. As time passed, North Omaha experienced a talent and brain drain, where our best and brightest escaped Omaha to find other places to manifest their potential. Many stayed but fled to West

Omaha. North Omaha was left with poverty, drained of talent, stripped of wealth, brains, and no tax base and with faced daily villainization, racism, and bigotry. Other invasions, including a freeway that divided the community, and a hotel that blocked off traffic flow to the area. With the police murder of innocent 14-year-old Vivian Strong, the city erupted in violence, leaving North Omaha in decay and economic chaos.

You are looking at the picture of systemic racism.

Since the 1960s, the North Omaha community has had no beneficial (strategic) investments. The lack of investment has produced the health disparities, mass incarceration, educational gaps (and separate-but-unequal school districts), biased policing, voter suppression, and wealth disparities that are plagues on our community. Meanwhile, the downtown skyline thrives, Midtown Crossing grows, the west sprawls, while heavy investment in north downtown dominates. Yet, North Omaha suffers from a generation of little investment, a lack of cultural sensitivity, and inequality. Even as subtle economic growth and development begins in North Omaha, black contractors and businesses do not benefit.

We are angry and demand change. We are sick and tired of racist acts against our community members, culminating with the murder of young James Scurlock. We continue to mourn Minnesota's George Floyd, and many other Blacks struck down. Yes, we call for justice, but we also call for strategic investment into North Omaha. An Omaha native, Malcolm X, said plainly, the Black man can do something to "give himself an independent economy" and "provide job opportunities for himself." We call for strategic investment into North Omaha.

In a June 2020 column, I called for the full community to listen first, then to learn and to act only on the recommendations coming from the communities affected. Join us in creating long-awaited changes, including my focus: strategic investment into North Omaha.

- Real change for North Omaha will start with investments
- The Economics of investments, financially and otherwise.
- Slavery (free labor) was the first jolt to the economics of black folks. Later came the massacres in Tulsa, Oklahoma (1921), and Rosewood, Florida (1923), and now the urban economic decay that includes North Omaha.

There is an undeniable interconnectivity of the effects of racism on the other calls for change, i.e., mass incarceration, joblessness, health disparities, housing ownership, mental health, educational gaps, and wealth disparity. If we can't fix racism but do fix wealth disparity, we will have an impact on all of the rest.

I'd like to share my recommended framework for short- and long-term investments in North Omaha that would:

- positively impact all of the disparities mentioned above
- reduce a percentage of the crime committed by those within the urban poverty cycle who look to crime as the only way to survive.

The investments need to come from the following citywide sectors.

Private sector, including corporate

Private corporations must evaluate the corporate culture as to its sensitivity and receptivity to diversity. Leaders, entrepreneurs, and managers must seek input from inside your organizations as well as from outside sources which are credible and trusted.

- Evaluate the diversity in the boardroom, executive suite, and management pipelines.

- Make commitments to buy business services, goods, and professional services from the vast number of small but capable businesses from the depressed North and South Omaha communities.

When constructing, ensure that the general contractor makes a concerted effort to include small subcontractors from the depressed communities of North and South Omaha. It is the owner of the project who sets the tone, and the beneficiaries of the construction can also provide support for inclusive hiring practices.

Evaluate opportunities for joint ventures, and invest in projects that benefit the growth of North and South Omaha.

Make a multimillion-dollar investment in entrepreneurship and support for black-led businesses and organizations. Commit to do business with black and North Omaha businesses.

Public Sector: federal, state, and local

1. Do a complete evaluation of the impediments to small and emerging businesses and make appropriate changes.
2. Seek representatives from the small and emerging business community to assist and get input regarding the challenges of doing business.
3. Understand the positive impact that doing business with small businesses can have on the depressed community.
4. Make a multimillion-dollar investment in the infrastructure in North Omaha, with incentives to recruit employers, homeownership, and housing renovations. Make street improvements, support entrepreneurship centers and incubators, arts and culture, and business districts along 24th, 30th and Ames corridors.

5. Develop a strategic economic development plan with the state.
6. Provide training opportunities in business, federal and state income and sales tax preparation, employment laws, and other critical programs to help business-minded individuals create and run prosperous business ventures.

Philanthropic/Foundation sector

In addition to the wonderful contributions that positively assist our community and its nonprofits, conduct a review that focuses on the organizations that are strategic to the health, cultural survival, growth, and survival of the impoverished community. So many of our very important nonprofits, while receiving assistance, are struggling to survive.

Invest in education, poverty alleviation, mental, and behavioral health supports, access to healthy food, cultural organizations and venues, early childhood education, housing developments, and support for wealth creation and ownership in struggling communities.

Financial sector

Our financial institutions must re-evaluate their presence as it relates to the Community Reinvestment Act and their strategic lending practices that could be directed toward the growth and survival of our community and small businesses.

North Omaha needs increased community development partners from our financial community.

- Investments support access to credit and capital to support small businesses, homeownership, down payment assistance, renovation and home improvement loans, workforce development and employment initiatives.
- Financial literacy programs provide stability for the community, and people of all ages—topics such as owning a home, investing, philanthropy, retirement, and social security decisions.

The return on investment, from all of the listed sectors, will include:

- A more self-sufficient and self-reliant North Omaha.
- Increase in disposable income that will stay, and be spent, within the community.
- An increase in community entrepreneurship and its impact on jobs.

- A reduction of talent and brain drain from the community.
- An increase in homeownership.
- An increase in the tax base: property, income, and sales.
- The ability of the community to support its nonprofits.
- The long-term development of wealth and self-sufficiency within the community.
- Direct positive linkage to existing negative social disparities.

The framework that we have outlined above is just that—a framework. Groups will articulate specific line-item investments from the North Omaha community, including the Empowerment Network's facilitated recommendations, and by many other groups joining them or coming forward. I hope that each of the sectors will understand and adopt this framework, and partner with the community on specific forthcoming recommendations. Adopting the framework is an immediate first-step action item.

AN ESSAY COLLECTION

Preamble: North Omaha's Bermuda Triangle

With the advent of Covid-19, extraordinary voids have been exposed in the development of the North Omaha community. Those voids are analogous to Bermuda Triangle. And as you know, it is said that items that fall into the infamous Bermuda Triangle never resurface.

So, you ask, what are the Omaha triangular pieces. I propose to you that they are:

**The strong need for unified community efforts
(Unity)**

**Community investment and development of wealth
(Wealth)**

**The passing of Will Brown and the resulting need for reconciliation
(Reconciliation)**

Unity

What the shock and trauma of Covid-19 has placed at the foot of the community is the challenge of letting the virus bring the community to its knees and forcing us to do the best we can to survive albeit, individually. After all, we needed to be fed, and employed, housed, staying safe, and saved. Of course, individually and as a people, we are survivors. After all, we survived slavery, racist policies, bigotry, redlining, lack of civil and voting rights. We can survive.

However, survival has always been better and achievable when we worked together. Need I remind us of the Underground Railroad, the Civil Rights Movement, marching in the streets, and quite frankly, even the phenomenon of Black Power. We do better surviving when we are responsible and unified in our approaches.

Now here comes this virus, North Omaha. As an elder in this community, I can report that this community is working collaboratively, collectively, and for the good of all, like never before. More specifically, we have never been more prepared to make a difference as a community than we are now. We have individuals—African American men and women—who are in positions of power and leverage in government, in private industries, in education, and organizations.

- We are feeding our kids from OPS.
- We are feeding our poor and elderly through churches and other organizations.
- We are servicing our unemployed and underemployed
- We are providing and organizing housing and shelter needs.
- We are providing for the unique health needs, physical and mental, through our health outlets in the community, our pastors, and neighborhoods.
- We are providing unique voter aides to open avenues for our people to vote in this important election. We are trying to prevent the result of stress and uncertainty through violence prevention and mental health counseling through our law enforcement and community organizations. We are providing our small businesses with loans
- We have created a Black Media Collaborative that is prime to spread the necessary messages for being safe and important news.
- We are providing these initiatives in a unified and collaborative way, led by the leadership of Willie Barney and so many others. The goal is to distribute some unique and important messages,

for the survival of our communities, from leaders who have built a platform to do that. That's the impact and lesson of unity.

Wealth

For a community to grow and survive, especially a community that is complex as to its residents, meaning we are no longer just African Americans. Still, Latino, Somalian, South Sudanese, Korean, Asian, and more, we are based in poverty, and we have a long history of disinvestment.

Investment means that in order for the community to grow and create wealth within, there needs to be public and private investment. That translates into jobs and opportunities for small businesses to grow, and, ultimately, the residual wealth that is within and stays within our community. New development in North Omaha that doesn't have residual community benefits is not the right kind of investment. It needs to be a community-beneficial investment that is understood and executed as such, and directed toward building community wealth. The virus has pointed out the void of wealth in our community. Our businesses were failing before, and now, during this virus—our organizations are struggling. Our nonprofits are struggling and dependent upon good-natured philanthropy and foundations. There is not enough wealth in the community to support our organizations and businesses. There is not enough wealth in the community to support small business stationarity and growth. May I note, a dependent community is not a strong community.

Reconciliation

With the commemoration of the 100th anniversary of the Will Brown lynching in 1919, and our associated memory of the lynching of Mr. George Smith, aka Joe Coe, we had a marvelous opportunity to finally come to grips with the horrible, racial history within our Omaha. That included violent racial events such as lynchings and more, such as redlining, discrimination as to public accommodations and private businesses, employment discrimination, health determinants and resulting disparities, educational retardation, unequal schools, and lack of teachers and administrators of color at all levels. We need to reconcile those disparities and impact, to make amends to restructure our thinking about diversity and equality, or we will never be able to have clarity on where we need to go, until we have clarity and honesty on where we have been. We missed the easy opportunity to begin the reconciliation process by using the dramatic Will Brown story to do so. We commemorated, but we did not begin reconciliation. After all, wasn't it the year of Jubilee?

Those three voids of our past—lack of unity, lack of wealth, and the lack of reconciliation—is our Bermuda Triangle. Now with the virus, that we have made a miraculous movement as it relates to unity, let us take this same opportunity to miraculously address the question of wealth and reconciliation for our beloved North Omaha.

So, I challenge us to realize that items that fall into the Bermuda Triangle never resurface. Let's defy that notion.

AN ESSAY COLLECTION

"Give me Liberty..."

Patrick Henry, in 1775, spoke to his fellow colonists and to the British when he said, "Give me liberty or give me death." Nearly 250 years later, I, too, scream for liberty. I make this appeal, not to the element of white supremacists and overt racists. I need not waste my time with that audience. Nor do I appeal to my more progressive, less racist white counterparts, who may share my anguish and pain as to our common view of the realities in America. My appeal is directed toward the large segment of our white American communities. These folks are well-meaning but seem to have amnesia when it comes to the history of white America and its treatment of its Black co-citizens.

Don't you remember that in 1865, in the 13th Amendment to our beloved Constitution, slavery was "abolished?" Yet for centuries, manipulation, via indentured servitude and more, minimized that Amendment. And you may have forgotten that slavery provided free labor to build this country and to build generational wealth for countless whites.

Don't you remember the 14th Amendment, which gave everybody equal protection and civil rights in this country in 1868? So, where did the idea of separate but equal come from? Where did separate water fountains and unequal schools come from after the enactment of the 14th Amendment?

Don't you remember, in 1870, the 15th Amendment to the Constitution that gave all the right to vote—as long as you were male? Yet John Lewis had his head beaten, and activists were assassinated nearly 100 years later, still advocating for that right.

Don't you remember the horrors of lynching well into the 1900s? As Americans, we should have been done with slavery, unequal rights under the law, and any impediments to voting by the end of the 19th century. We should have been done with taking the breath and lives of our fellow man over the right to have our voices heard. But it never stopped. It took the brutal, vicious, and long civil rights movement to push for the truth of those Amendments. The horror of opposition followed in the form of Jim Crowism and more.

Is America asking the African American also to have amnesia, not to remember these horrible deeds, and for us to ignore our memory of America and its promises, its amendments and its deeds?

We counter the amnesia of white Americans with the historical and institutional memory of the African American. Need I remind you that law enforcement officers populated the Ku Klux Klan? The beating of John Lewis was by law enforcement officers. Law enforcement officers perpetrated the killing of key civil rights workers in Mississippi. A beautiful 14-year-old, poverty-stricken, innocent black girl named Vivian Strong was shot in the back of the head by a police officer in Omaha.

To be clear, we know the vast majority of police are good people dedicated to their job. But death by the police is nothing new. Are you asking us Black folks to forget? Black people have institutional knowledge of all of that, regardless of their age. It is instilled in them by their fathers, mothers, and grandparents.

So, in 2020, after years of killings by rogue police officers all over this country, culminated by George Floyd's death, and punctuated by the shooting of Jacob Blake, if you have amnesia, then you may be surprised at our sustained anger. Plain and simple, you cannot separate the past injustices by claiming amnesia or indifference.

After the Civil War, called the Reconstruction period, there was great hope because of the 13th, 14th, and 15th Amendments. But along came Jim Crow. In the middle and late 1960s, there was great hope with the passage of new civil rights laws. Then came the "new" attitude of African Americans, declaring that enough was enough, and America erupted with the race riots and civil disobedience.

In response to the unrest, African Americans saw exponential growth in elected office and movement within corporate America. We had hope again. We even began to run for President: Shirley Chisholm in 1972, Jesse Jackson in 1984, and many others to follow. We saw economic growth in sectors of the Black community, mostly in entertainment and athletics, and even the election of a Black man to the United States Presidency. We had not forgotten the past, but we had hope again. Then came a steep increase in racial divisiveness, and white supremacy reached its highest level, followed by more rogue police killings of our Black people.

White Americans may have amnesia as to what has happened, but don't ask us to forget. We're demanding reforms in policing and change in all segments of society. The well of hope is running dry. My message should be clear. Despite my institutional historical memory, should we again have hope? Or will we have more of the same? "Black Lives Matter" signs abound, but should we have hope of sustained change and reform?

Give me liberty. Together, let's convert hope into healing and real progress. Improve your memory so that I can reduce mine.

── AN ESSAY COLLECTION ──

BLACKS AND THE VACCINE

Matthew 25:40: "Verily I say unto you, in as much as you have done it onto one of the least of these, my Brethren, ye have done it unto me."

Over the past months, I have written about the need for Whites to listen, learn, and recognize the plight, anger, and demands of people of color. Uniquely, 2020 provided many opportunities for that journey toward clarity and, hopefully, participation in needed reform. Specifically, the teaching opportunities in 2020 were presented by George Floyd's death, the rise in White supremacy, and, dramatically and tragically, COVID-19.

No other example is more pungent than the reluctance of people of color to take the COVID-19 vaccine. In September, I wrote an article entitled "White America may have amnesia, but don't ask Blacks to forget," which also served as an introduction to the thought of Blacks being reluctant to take the vaccine.

Blacks have many reasons to be distrustful of public health guidance. Beyond slavery and all of its residuals, Blacks remember the *Tuskegee Study*. For 40 years, beginning in 1932, under the direction of federal health officials, African Americans were given injections of syphilis without their permission or awareness. By the mid-1940s, penicillin had been proven as an effective treatment for the disease, but men in the study were not offered the cure.

In other instances, during the 1918 flu pandemic, Blacks routinely were denied health care thanks to Jim Crow racist policies that lasted into the 1980s. Black women in Mississippi were sterilized, without their permission, to prevent the birth of Black children. Flint, Michigan, recently joined a settlement for $641 million over lead levels in the water of the majority poor and Black city.

American's longstanding disparities in health delivery, death rates of people of color, captured in myriad studies over the years, are part of the problem of economic disparity among people of color in America. And we simply cannot overlook the mistrust that has been generated by the lies and misinformation about the corona virus from the previous administration.

I could continue, but I hope we can agree to acknowledge the distrust and reluctance of African Americans to take the vaccine. We don't trust the "system." According to a Kaiser Health study, "over 35% of Blacks either don't or probably won't see themselves, as taking the vaccine." Of those Blacks, 71% attributed this to distrust.

Despite the distrust, I believe there is a viable path for African Americans to evaluate and embrace the vaccine. First, it also needs to be acknowledged that unless approximately 75% of Americans get the vaccine, the effectiveness for our country will be severely retarded.

Secondly, we have to be clear about the dangers of not taking the vaccine. We all know someone who has succumbed to COVID-19. Without the vaccine, more people will die. Tuskegee was a trick using Black folks as guinea pigs. This is not the case for the COVID-19 vaccine — everyone is being asked to take it.

Finally, instead of the virus subsiding, we are in another surge and don't have the luxury to ignore the reality of this virus and its more virulent permutations.

For all African Americans who have a reluctance, I suggest the following path:

Analyze the data, follow the science of the vaccine's impact and safety, and use our trusted and credible sources to evaluate it with them. For the record, Dr. Kizzmekia Corbett was an African American lead scientist in the development of the vaccine. Additionally, we have numerous trusted African Americans in our community's health care delivery system. Furthermore, African Americans are part of all groups in line for early distribution, including medical personnel, first responders, the elderly, and people in group settings. These groups have already begun to receive the vaccine.

We, the community, have a responsibility to demand that our trusted sources make their recommendations known. I am confident that our community experts will alert us to any concerns stemming from the vaccine. I will take the vaccine as soon as my turn comes up. Also, make sure we practice safe measures now, during, and after your inoculations.

Given the history of disparities, we must hold the state and county responsible for distributing the vaccine in an equitable way to communities of color in subsequent phases. We must hold them accountable, and they must distribute equitably.

May readers learn from this teaching opportunity, not only about Blacks' reluctance to the vaccine but also about Blacks' lack of trust in the system that continues to consciously and unconsciously enforce disparities across institutions. Disparities are measurable in mass incarceration, policing, education equality, economic development, and health care affordability and availability. Become an ambassador for equality. Demand change and reform in policies, programs and institutions in all levels of government.

AN ESSAY COLLECTION

JOHN LEWIS:
THE FIRST AND THE LAST

Congressman John Lewis was a friend of mine for forty years. With the advent of his death, I feel compelled to share my perspective on my dear friend. John Lewis was 80 years old.

In 1980, after having moved to Atlanta, I became a part of the inner circle of the Civil Rights community in Atlanta, Georgia. Later, I became the Director of Budget for the City of Atlanta, appointed by former Ambassador and then Mayor of the City of Atlanta, Andrew Young. John Lewis was a newly elected member of the Atlanta City Council, and I was a Lieutenant for Mayor Young.

I had additional responsibilities to "whip" the city council for the Mayor. May I digress to say a "whip" is one who would get the Council members whipped in line for the Mayor as it relates to their vote and their support of issues initiated or advocated by the Mayor. So, my reflections and perspectives on John Lewis first occurred in that capacity.

But before we move on, let me provide a historical perspective of Lewis at that time in his life. By 1980, John Lewis had become a Civil Rights icon. Earlier in 1965, John was nearly beaten to death, on the Edmund Pettus Bridge, during the first of three infamous marches from Selma to Montgomery. Please note that as a result, later that year, the awesome 1965 Voting Rights Act was passed.

For the young readers, may I say that the Selma marches, were peaceful protest marches demanding change and reform, (albeit for voting rights). A quick historical note: In 2013, the U.S. Supreme Court gutted the 1965 Voting Act (Shelby vs Holder). "Deja Vu all over again." I remind you that John Lewis was the youngest, and maybe the second-most electric speaker at the 1963 March on Washington? John Lewis was **the first** young African American to be known to lead, and to stand up for social justice, at that march. In 1963, John Lewis was 18 years old... Additionally, John Lewis tirelessly, and fearlessly worked in the dangerous southern states to register African Americans to vote, along with another civil rights icon.

Before we return to my experience with John Lewis in the early 1980s, let me identify John's partner in the agonizing voter registration efforts mentioned above during his tenure as Atlanta City Councilman. He is also a very dear friend of mine, the renowned, late Julian Bond.

Continuing, I want to share with you the impossible job I had occasionally, attempting to persuade John Lewis to cast his city council vote with Mayor Young, who he loved. When John felt that it did not pass his test of what was righteous for the people, meaning no political maneuvers, no political deal, his response was a stern No. No, unless it adhered to John's sense of what he felt was right, he would not vote with anyone, including the Mayor.

For me, as the Mayor's whip, it was a horrible job sometimes, but when we walked away, we always left with the highest respect for John Lewis. That was John Lewis as a councilman and then as a Congressman. No Nancy Pelosi nor any other political giant could sway John away from his principles.

John never changed. He was the rock, he was the conscience of the Atlanta City Council and the conscience of the United States House of Representatives for 44 years.

When I reflect on John Lewis and my experiences with him, many names pop up in my head. They include Civil Rights icon C.T. Vivian (who also died July 17), 88-year-old Mayor Andrew Young, my dear friend Coretta Scott King, and more. But one remaining name that comes to mind when I think of John, that name, the aforementioned Julian Bond.

By 1985, my friend John Lewis and my friend Julian Bond decided to run for Congress—and it was against each other. They were dear and close friends. Julian Bond was hands down the favorite to win the race. John was iconic and historic; Julian was charismatic, handsome, an eloquent speaker, and extremely intelligent. Julian was the favorite. So, Preston Love Jr., who had just returned home from running Jesse Jackson's presidential race in 1984, was the sought-after advisor by both campaigns. What a dilemma for me. I loved them both, but I chose Julian Bond. There were several other people in the race, which required a run-off.

In the primary, Julian received the most votes. John Lewis won the race. I won an egg on my face.

While John never let me forget that in the early days. He was a man of such high character, he continued to embrace our friendship—mine and Julian's. It's important to note that John Lewis was elected 22 times for that same seat until he died.

I hope that John Lewis's life serves as a beacon to our young, because John spent his whole life fighting for change and reform, and he said over and over, "Never give up. It's going to be tough, but never give up. And if you stay with it, you will win the fight." So, on behalf of John Lewis to our young folks who I join in their calls for change in every way, I hope that they follow John's mantra and never give up.

I caution that our young generation, as well as our older generations, strive to see the leverage of registering and voting. I say boldly and strongly as a veteran of the many years and cycles of racial disparities, and lack of equity, that in November of 2020, we all need to VOTE LIKE CRAZY. And when we do, we honor John Lewis, **who was the first, and true to the very last.**

RIP

AN ESSAY COLLECTION

Context, Compassion in the Poindexter Case

In this chapter, I write about another friend whose life and experiences make him a symbol for the complexity of criminal justice in America—Ed Poindexter.

Ed Poindexter and I grew up in the infamous public homes known as Logan Fontenelle. Some of Omaha's most significant and influential people grew up there—the very long list includes Baseball Hall of Famer Bob Gibson and media executive Cathy Hughes—the wealthiest Black woman in America, besides Oprah.

Logan Fontenelle was at the center of the most segregated section of the city, North Omaha, and full of African Americans who had migrated from the American South for packing house jobs. Ed Poindexter grew up in the courtyards of Logan Fontenelle in the late '40s and early '50s.

While many African American youths quickly left North Omaha in what could be called a migration of talent, brains, and economic base, not everyone could. I was able to exit, but Ed did not.

Nationally and locally, having endured racism, Jim Crowism, redlining and more, African Americans began to evolve toward a positive community self-awareness and resistance to racism. Products of this environment were Afro hairstyles, calls of "Black is beautiful," activism, Black Power, and self-determinism.

It's important to know that African Americans of all ages have an institutional memory—either by direct experience or family lore—that includes slavery, lynching, racism and its manifestations. White people must understand that Black history is dominated by law enforcement and intimidation, whether via the Ku Klux Klan, police, sheriffs or others. History is not erased easily. So when we talk about George Floyd, we are not talking about something new. Our institutional memory of law enforcement is critical to appreciate.

The largest domestic law enforcement institution in America is the FBI, under the leadership of J. Edgar

Hoover from 1924-72. It may be difficult for some readers to acknowledge, but the FBI played significant roles in the destruction, the deaths, the manipulation, and the discrediting of many African Americans, especially during the '60s and '70s. The FBI considered these organizations and their leaders potential threats to America: the Southern Christian Leadership Conference, led by Martin Luther King Jr.; Malcolm X and his organizations; and the Black Panthers. The FBI's actions included infiltration, disruption and a counterintelligence effort, COINTELPRO.

During this time, we had civil rights organizations in several layers in Omaha, as was the case nationally. We had a robust Black clergy, who led many or most of the calls for change and reform, we had a local chapter of the NAACP, we had the St. Martin de Porres Club, and we had chapters of the Black Panther Party. The Black Panther Party, of which Ed Poindexter was a member, was known for community outreach, including food programs, breakfast programs for youths, youth cultural education and history programs, patrols against police violence, speeches, newsletters, and programs directed toward training and education for the community. After intensive attacks nationally on the Black Panthers and disruptions by COINTELPRO, no new chapters were being approved and most were being ordered to disband. In Omaha, the Black Panther Party discontinued and went under the name the National Committee to Combat Fascism (NCCF).

In 1969, an Omaha police officer shot a 14-year-old girl in the back of the head at Logan Fontenelle Homes. Her name was Vivian Strong. She and several girlfriends had been accused of playing their music too loudly and ran when the police arrived. The reaction in North Omaha was rioting and renewed anger against the police.

Against this backdrop, in 1970, Ed Poindexter and friend David Rice, members of the NCCF, were accused of orchestrating a bombing that killed policeman Larry Minard and injured another officer. They were convicted and sentenced to life.

I believe that David Rice, who died in prison, and Ed Poindexter, who remains imprisoned, are innocent. We view them as political prisoners of an unwarranted focus on racial activism.

Numerous attempts to have the evidence reviewed and challenged have been dismissed. But never has the Black community discounted the

Minard family's pain and suffering. In recent days, I have spoken to members of the Minard family and felt their anger about their loved one's death. My heart, and the hearts of so many, go out to the family. My effort here to focus attention on the plight of Ed Poindexter does not diminish our compassion for the Minard family.

Ed Poindexter is 75 years old and in ill health. A small team is seeking to have Ed released, based on his medical condition and for compassion toward a person who has had an exemplary record inside the prison system. This team, along with attorney Tim Ashford, seeks to complete the legal framework needed to bring Ed Poindexter's case before the Nebraska Board of Pardons.

In late July, we conducted a prayer vigil at Clair Memorial United Methodist Church. Ten pastors prayed for forgiveness, unity, mercy, reform, the Vivian Strong family, the Minard family, James Scurlock's family, the Poindexter family, and healing. It was live-streamed to hundreds across the city.

I pray, via this article, that the community will support this compassionate request for the release of Ed Poindexter.

— AN ESSAY COLLECTION —

King's dream is not achieved as Nebraska carries out assaults on Democracy

I reflect on the iconic speech of Dr. Martin Luther King Jr. in the summer of 1963, where he spoke of his famous dream. Embedded in that wonderful soliloquy are the dreams of freedom, justice and equality. All dreams have a commonality: The dreamer wakes up.

Well, I wake up in Nebraska nearly 70 years later, searching for Democracy in the state in which I was born and raised. I rub my eyes and finish my wake-up yawn and stretching, and translate King's dream into the hope that when wide awake, I will find Democracy in Nebraska. Democracy has its derivatives, but the core of Democracy in this country is the right to vote and the expectation of fairness throughout the voting process.

I am wide awake, and I am dismayed.

I was raised in a segregated, redlined, discriminated-against community, overlaid by layers of racism and bigotry, in my Nebraska. We have endured lynchings, killings by law enforcement, mass incarceration, race-based health disparities, educational gaps and disinvestment, and racial disrespect. I have lived, studied and written on the American history of centuries of voting impediments and violence, forced upon my race repeatedly.

Don't forget the hope brought on by the 15th Amendment to the Constitution, removing race as a barrier to register to vote, and the 1965 Voting Rights Act, which again, removed race-based barriers to voting. But despite all of that, each of those instances met the oppressive forces of Jim Crow, hostile Supreme Court decisions, and an aggressive group of states and forces opposing true Democracy, mainly because of race and privilege. Dr. King dreamt, but now we need reality to set in.

Unfortunately, the reality is that Nebraska is undermining Democracy.

Nebraska undermines Democracy when Attorneys General in 17 states, including Nebraska, supported Texas's lawsuit that called for overturning election results favoring Joe Biden in Georgia, Pennsylvania, Wisconsin and Michigan. Two of the U.S. House members from Nebraska also supported the lawsuit. It was frivolous, an affront to all Nebraska voters, and surely the voters of color in those states, and the voters of color in our state.

There is no coincidence, but after the strong African American vote throughout this country for Barack Obama in 2008, the reaction from red states, including Nebraska, was to create measures to try to minimize and suppress future African American votes. What emerged was Legislation to force voters to present I.D. to fix phantom fraud, a disguise for the suppression of people of color. Voter ID presents problems for many other classes of people. Many red states enacted those voter I.D. laws, and as expected, suppression of votes is occurring. Nebraska undermines Democracy when it tries over and over, year after year, failure after failure, to pass voter I.D. requirements. The question is, "What's the problem?"

The answer is, it's an assault on Democracy.

After the 2010 census, the 2nd Congressional District was politically gerrymandered to prevent another victory like Obama's—successfully watering down the Black vote in Congressional District 2. Fast forward to 2020. An extraordinarily high vote gave another victory in District 2 to the Democratic presidential candidate.

Now, with redistricting again approaching, people of color in Nebraska request an independent drawing and review of the congressional district lines, to stop gerrymandering that would further water down the Black vote. African Americans, request passage of the Redistricting Act for Democracy's sake.

In all states other than Nebraska and Maine, "winner take all" provisions are in place, awarding all of a state's electoral votes to go to the winner of the state, regardless of congressional district vote totals. Nebraska and Maine allow individual electoral votes to go to the winner of each congressional district.

So, as Obama did in 2008, Biden won the single vote from Nebraska's Congressional District 2 in the 2020 election. It is no coincidence that immediately, there were calls to eliminate that ability, and return to the unfair "winner take all" technique.

On Feb. 17, I found myself testifying at three Legislative hearings:

- L.B. 76, returning to the "winner take all" awarding of electoral votes—a potential assault on Democracy.
- LR3CA, a constitutional amendment to require voter I.D.—a potential assault on Democracy.
- And LB107, adopting a fair Redistricting Act—a protection against an assault on Democracy.

I challenge the State of Nebraska to recognize that these proposals to suppress the votes of many, and in particular, people of color, are assaults on Democracy in our state. Nebraska needs an awakening.

—— AN ESSAY COLLECTION ——

The Horrible Cycle of Voter Suppression

The 15th Amendment gave all males the right to vote regardless of race, color or previous conditions of slavery. That happened in 1870. In response and almost immediately, Blacks began to register and vote in record numbers. Our history books chronicle in the years following the 1870s, 1880s and 1890s, there was an incredible surge of Black Elected Officials (BEOs), that included a few United States Senators, and dozens of Black members of the House of Representatives. These victories were won in the South because of the large number of Blacks in the Southern states. By the way, that surge in BEOs correlated with a period in American history for Black Americans called Reconstruction, where Blacks flourished in civics, culture, arts, and education.

After the success of Blacks voting, we entered the first full cycle of pushback. Jim Crow voter suppression. The pushback on voter participation by Blacks included the loss of power and privilege to Blacks. That cycle of voter suppression entered into new aggression, which took the form of legal and de facto measures. These included literacy tests, poll taxes, grandfather clauses, gerrymandering, employer intimidation, countless silly measures like having to name the number of jelly beans in a jar, and lastly, unbridled violence and deaths. Jim Crowism and voter suppression flourished against Blacks for decades. Beginning in the 1940s and in earnest in the mid-1950s, Blacks declared that enough was enough. What evolved was the civil rights movement.

Besides civil rights, the full civil rights movement fought against the voter suppression measures throughout the Southern states. Blacks simply wanted to register and be able to vote. Many Blacks were victims of violence and death to gain the rights afforded by the 15th Amendment. May I interject a historical note? In 1920, the 19th Amendment gave all women the right to vote, albeit African American women were now faced with the same challenge as African American men: to make the constitutional amendments real.

In 1965, John Lewis, Martin Luther King, Jr., and many others brought the fight for voting rights to light by marching across the Edmund Pettus Bridge to demonstrate for the right to vote in Alabama. That included Bloody Sunday, where the marchers were beaten unmercifully and killed. The images of the violence against the marchers in the media helped to facilitate the passage of the 1965 Voting Rights Act. That Act was the most significant advance in voting rights for all people, but specifically for Blacks. It made illegal all of the Jim Crow suppression measures that were instituted by the Southern states. It not only made suppression illegal, but it also gave the government, specifically the Justice Department, the power to challenge any known voter suppression attempts. Sections of the law also forced nine of those Southern states to obtain approval from the Justice Department before any changes to the voting procedures in their states that could be potential hindrances or suppressions were enacted.

After the passage of the Act, Black voters once again turned out in record numbers, and BEO numbers soared to new heights. Blacks were elected all over the country, including the Southern states, as mayors, local officials, governors, and to the U.S. Senate and

Congress. And once again, the reaction of Whites to the loss of power, privilege, and control fostered repeated attempts to negate the powers of the 1965 Voting Rights Act.

One of the positive impacts of the 1965 Voting Rights Act was the first Black woman, Shirley Chisholm, to run as a candidate for President in 1972, and the first Black man to run for president in modern times, Jessie Jackson, in 1984. (Full disclosure: I was his campaign organizer and first director.) And lastly, the victory of Barack Obama in 2008.

The repeated attempts to dismantle the 1965 Voter Rights Act by Republicans was finally successful in a big way in 2013, when a Supreme Court ruling (Shelby vs. Holder), dismantled the power of the 1965 Voting Rights Act under the guise that since Obama had won the 2008 race, there was no longer any voter suppression. The horrible cycle of voter suppression reemerged. Republicans returned to the measures of the Jim Crow era and began to institute some of the old voter suppression techniques of the past, but also introduced new ones, such as purging of the voter files, requiring voter I.D., the closing of polling locations, and more.

Enter 2020. Record turnout in voter participation nationwide and Democratic victories catapults the ugly cycle of voter suppression attempts to a fever pitch. Now in 2021, we find that 44 states, including Nebraska, have instituted over 200 voter suppression initiatives. The State of Georgia has become the poster state for voter suppression. After the Jim Crow suppressions of the late 1800s and the 1965 Voting Rights Act, a new list of voter suppression measures emerged: reduction of voting hours, laws and rules to reduce of use of early voting and voting-by-mail, tampering with the postal service, reducing the number of voter drop boxes, aggressive misinformation, reduction of the polling places to force long lines, and in Georgia, passed a law prohibiting access to water to prevent people standing in line to vote in sweltering heat. And one more thing, many states are giving the legislatures the right to challenge—and possibly undo—valid election results.

In 2021, we are left with the memory, observation, and study of this vicious, horrible cycle of voter suppression; we are left with the responsibility of the democracy-minded, to fight back this challenge to Democracy in the United States and in Nebraska. There are two major pieces of Legislation, which once again we need to step up support and stop the flood of voter suppression. Democrats, Republicans, and Independents all need to be on the front lines to fight the battle of voter suppression by aggressively supporting two national pieces of Legislation:

- the John Lewis Voting Rights Act, which restores the lost powers of the 1965 Voting Rights Act, and
- House Bill HR1, which enhances many measures to make voting easier for everybody.

And in Nebraska, let's all urge our state senators to remove Nebraska from the list of states trying to continue the horrible cycle of voter suppression. That's "The good life" people of color are seeking!

AN ESSAY COLLECTION

Racism's Tug-of-War with Democracy

In my last essay, I spoke about the horrible cycle of voter suppression. Since the writing of that piece, we all have been faced with a manifestation of evidence of the point. Since that article was written, the state of Georgia has created the most bizarre and horrible evidence of how far voter suppression has come. And, many of our states appear to be moving to join Georgia, including Florida and Arizona. Florida on the front end and Arizona on the back end.

Florida has introduced new techniques to restrict voting; in particular to restrict use of drop-boxes and vote-by-mail. Arizona seeks to overturn their results by recounting and attempting to challenge the 2020 vote in their state. Georgia, the current leader of voter suppression in the nation, claims that they are making voting easier by changing their laws. These claims are both not true and laughable. The Georgia law will limit usage of vote-by-mail and drop-boxes, reduce early voting times and mechanisms, and remove the Secretary of State from being a voting member on the Election Board and unbelievably, this would give the state legislature the power to suspend an election result. May I remind us all that the Georgia Secretary of State refused to bow down to the former president's request to find more than 11,000 votes on his behalf? Let us not forget that bringing water or food to voters who are forced to stand for hours in line to vote, has been made illegal, albeit that the lines were longer *because* of the new statutes that create long lines.

All of this brings us to the necessity to further look at this voter suppression tug of war, which is rooted in racism, preservation of power, and political demagoguery. At the other side of the tug of war, pulls Democracy. Voting is an expression of individual liberty. Our founders saw that governments exist to protect our inalienable rights, of which voting is one. The Constitution doesn't guarantee the right to vote, it states that the government cannot deny or abridge our rights.

Historically, efforts to abridge those rights have been mitigated—like a tug-of-war to stop racism and preservation of power—and let us not forget that the rights of Black and other people of color were abridged in 1857, by the Dred Scott Supreme Court decision and abridged by Jim Crow, in overt and de-facto ways, and again abridged with the Supreme Court decision in 2013, in Shelby v. Holder. Those abridgments created a tug-of-war between those attempts and the Civil War, the 13th, 14th, 15th and 19th amendments, as well as the 1964 Civil Rights Act and the 1965 Voting rights act.

So, we find ourselves in 2021, with an all-out, renewed, unbridled attack, to abridge our voting rights, with Georgia leading the charge. This time the tug of war is led by the forces of political demagoguery and racism. What we are faced with is for us to not be fooled by nice and democratic statements and pleads of misinformation about what these new attempts really are. They are directed to change the political vote by suppression and to maintain political power. It is not issue-based; it is about survival of political demagoguery.

So, the tug-of-war continues, and on the other side of those fighting for suppression, are three major pieces of Legislation:

1. <u>The for the People Act</u>, (H.R.1/S.1), 2021. To date, 47 states have introduced more than 360 bills aimed at abridging our ability to vote. H.R.1/S.1 will expand access to the ballots, override most of the various state's voter suppression legislation and include:

- Automatic voter registration
- At least 2 weeks of early voting
- No discriminatory voter I.D.
- Restore voting rights upon release from prison
- Make election day a holiday

2. <u>The John Lewis Voting Rights Advancement Act</u> of 2021 (H.R.4) This Act will restore the full power of the 1965 Voting Rights Act, dismantled by the 2013 Supreme Court, which includes the power to block racially discriminatory laws before they are enacted.

- Sets new criteria for states with histories of voter suppression
- Allows courts to block discriminatory election policies
- Ensures that new election rules comply with Supreme Court Ruling

3. <u>The Washington, D.C. Admission Act of 2021</u> (H.R.51/S.51). This bill will allow Washington D.C. to become the 51st state, and afford D.C. residents full representation in Congress.

- Will add two United States Senators
- Will add at least one member to the House of Representatives
- Will add a governor and all assets afforded to all states

---- AN ESSAY COLLECTION ----

Lessons from My Journey
(A Call to Action)

In the 2020 general election, I had a special opportunity to observe my Nebraska communities from a unique viewpoint.

As a Democrat, African American, in a predominately Republican state, and as a candidate (U.S. Senate), whose candidacy spanned a short 50 days, raised less than $5,000.00, and failed to have the time to create a campaign structure, my candidacy was unique, to say the least. I submit that my candidacy provided me with an opportunity to see what maybe no other has seen; the complexity, the frailties, and yet potential of our time in this very splintered world. The uniqueness of my journey provided me with the ability to observe, with my eyes and my mind, our Nebraska communities—in all of our rawness.

My campaign theme was simple, and intended to have a charm/cleverness, by the use of my name, with the theme, saying that "There Needs to be Love in the Senate." But, with the evolution of the campaign and my observation, that declaration of the need for love became profound, serious, and a needed mantra. May I offer from my lofty view, the following evidential dynamics of the 2020 election's <u>uniqueness/distinctiveness</u>:

1. The significant impact of the Covid-19 pandemic, driving a significant desire of voters to avoid in-person voting at the polls, or even focus on the rigors, dangers, and responsibility of voting.
2. The impact of the leader of our executive branch of government, no matter what your party affiliation, pro or con to Trump, I would guess that we all can agree that the injection of misinformation, lack of truth, and personal-tics instead of politics, may have contributed to this election and this uniqueness.
3. The re-emergence of what could be called "The New Jim Crow of Voter Suppression" including:

- Targeted purging of voter rolls
- Tampering and affecting the postal service delivery of voter mail
- Increased voter intimidation
- The undermining of voter confidence in the voting process
- The rampant reduction of polling places
- The rampant reduction in drop boxes
- Fake drop boxes
- The use of the court system to negate public voting
- The prediction that the election was going to be "fixed"
- A nation divided among racial lines and raw racism
- A test of Democracy

4. Racial division, captured in the concept of Black Lives Matter, death of Blacks by police and manifested in the heightened demand for justice, change and reform, and fueled by the rise of white supremacists, and also anarchists, who would love to see the races not only divide, but go to war and tear this country to shreds.

Anyone of these unique factors, contributing to the environment of the 2020 election, could be significant alone, but in the aggregate, they represented a potential catastrophic, and the most unique election in the history of our nation.

To be a candidate for the United States Senate in the midst of all the historic and unique election elements was personally a strange destiny. I want to share clarity that arose from this complex matrix of factors, as well as my viewpoint. Said simply, there is a great human need for hope, healing, reconciliation of our differences, and yes, love. That's part of my lesson from my journey. But there is more.

During my journey, I interacted with, spoke with, and observed horrible stress, mental health, and pain from the communities all over Nebraska because of COVID, poverty, lack of jobs, lack of food, lack of knowledge of available resources, or the lack of knowledge about available resources, health disparities, incarceration and inequities, all contributing the growth of hopelessness. A bitter lesson.

There is this real world beneath a campaign. Whether it be the campaign for United States Senate, or any other office, the realities are sitting there waiting for attention. Campaigns focus on attack ads, wonderful television advertising of make-believe, raising and spending vast amounts of money, and mostly overlooking or not focusing on the deep real-world needs of many.

Another lesson confirmed from my journey: The need to change. It was entirely unpredictable that my humble moneyless and challenging write-in campaign would receive a Nebraska record-breaking 62,000 write-in votes. It is remarkable, but clear, that my votes represented a peephole into the hearts and minds of many who used my campaign as a way to cry out. A cry to campaigns: You don't need to waste money, and waste the voters' time attacking and spending. And that, in spite of the all the unique factors to retard voting, they voted and voted in record numbers as a sign—a cry out help. If we as communities do not address the cries now, sexism, injustice, racism, hate, and poverty will reign supreme.

A Call to Action:

Public, Private and grassroots sector Leadership. We need to stop dancing around solutions to the raw needs and find solutions to the change and reforms. Together we can close the gaps of jobs, injustice, divisiveness, disparities, opportunity, equity, and inclusion. Come together, committed but knowing there is struggle in change. Reach out to credible and trusted sources. I suggest we take a mental inventory of how far we have come and how little progress we've actually made since the last breath of George Floyd.

I will also say this in closing, that in words of James Weldon Johnson, creator of the anthem, *"Lift Every Voice and Sing,"* we should *"Sing a song full of the faith that the dark past has taught us,"* and *"Sing a song full of the hope that the present has brought us."*

Let's make history.

| AN ESSAY COLLECTION |

Summer 2021 is time to celebrate Black culture once again

After more than a year of unbelievable stress and divisiveness, hate and overt racism toward people of color, we find ourselves in this Summer of 2021. We lift our heads above those realities to celebrate and embrace our wonderful Black and African American cultures.

The African American culture is rooted in African culture, but for over 400 years, our distinct African American culture has survived and evolved into something wonderful to behold. That culture is found in our remarkable and unique foods, and our diverse music (including slave songs, spirituals, blues, jazz, rhythm and blues, hip hop, rap, and more). It includes our rich commitment to the spiritual, comprising many denominations and religions; our art, including performing arts and visual arts, spoken word and written word; a rich history of scholars; and an elaborate fabric of social groups; our intercollegiate sororities and fraternities; all rooted in some form in the African American culture.

All of this is on full display in our Black communities, including my beloved North Omaha. These communities have endured all forms of slavery, lynchings, redlining, bigotry, overt racism, generations of voter suppression and poverty—and yet, have endured and produced. Our culture is a product of our history and a testimonial to our people and their strength and resolve.

Which brings us, again, to the wonderful display of our culture this summer. You can find our people enjoying summer by going to and cooking in the park, feasting on our wonderful food dishes, and social gatherings galore.

On June 19th, many celebrations will remember what is called Juneteenth. June 19, 1865, was the day word finally reached slaves in Galveston, Texas, that they had been freed via the Emancipation Proclamation, which was signed in January 1863.

The slaves began to celebrate their freedom. The celebrations took many names over the years, including Freedom Day and Emancipation Day, among others. Though initially celebrated in Galveston, Juneteenth has become a national celebration day for African Americans, including throughout North Omaha.

Racism, redlining, and lack of opportunities in Omaha forced a generation of young people, including myself, to flee to other cities, mostly west and north, to seek better opportunities and a better life. This took a tremendous toll on North Omaha and its potential—a brain drain of some of our most talented African Americans and their financial potential.

While the escape was comprehensive, many returned home to North Omaha during the holidays of summer. That evolved into a tradition that is known as Native Omaha Days in July for celebrations with friends and families. This wonderful display of African American culture often includes family and class reunions. This year the "Days" begin in the last week of July, centered at 24th and Lake.

Down the road in December, African Americans celebrate Kwanzaa, an annual seven-day celebration Dec. 26-Jan. 1, that focuses on unity, creativity, faith, and giving, and celebrates our culture.

Each summer, my organization, Black Votes Matter, conducts an annual six-day, all-expenses-paid tour for Omaha high school youth. We visit Memphis, Jackson, Birmingham, Tuskegee, Selma, Montgomery, and Atlanta to teach and expose our youth to their history and their culture, and hope that they learn and respect it. These participants then return home to become leaders who stay here and prosper.

This year the tour will leave July 11, carrying 40 of our youth and 20 adults. Please note the wisdom of the Omaha Public Schools, in that 10 OPS principals will join the tour for two days. It is my contention that a better understanding by all of the richness, contribution, and potential of the various cultures serves to mitigate white supremacy, hate, and even all forms of divisiveness that we are faced with in our country today.

'They watched us pray' — Omaha youth visit Southern civil rights sites

August 8, 2021, Updated September 14, 2021

We began on a beautiful Sunday evening with a large group of parents, family, friends, and supporters in a wonderful send-off. In some cases, young people were leaving the nest for the very first time. The anticipation among the youths varied, from, "Wow, I'm getting away from the house!" to, "Wow, I'm going to find out the truth about my history!"

Traveling in a 54-passenger charter bus trailed by a 12-passenger van, we shoved off to Memphis, Tennessee. My observation of the youth on board was that I had a very diverse group: Jewish, African, Latina, Caucasian, and African American. They had very diverse perceptions of what to expect, but very low knowledge of true African American history and an unrealistic view of the impact of this experience on their lives.

This year, year four of my tour for young Omahans of civil rights sites in the South provided a distinct look at the impact on the teens of the COVID-19 era, rampant misinformation, and the unleashing of new White supremacy.

I wondered what we would encounter with six intensive days and 40 teenagers exposed to all of these variables. Would it matter who Martin Luther King really was? Or John Lewis? Or Medgar Evers? Would it matter that their fellow man was hanged from a tree? Would it matter that because of race, human beings were not allowed full citizenship, denied equal opportunities, and murdered at will, without redress? Would it matter that their ancestors were phenomenal people who endured the past of America, who demanded and fought for equal rights, voting, and more? And with so many other areas to grab their attention, would we be able to gather their focus, for them to learn their history, the truth--the good, the bad, and the ugly of their past?

After arriving in Memphis, we got a hint at the answers. Their attention span was short, their need to know was lacking, the burdens of their life situations were stifling their blooming, their gifts, and their aspirations. That's what we thought we saw before day one. But we watched them peer into the room where Martin Luther King Jr. slept the night before being assassinated. We thought we saw a glimmer of focus.

We woke the next morning preparing to proceed to Jackson, Mississippi, and all of its horrible racial history. But we were faced with the reality of a near-death of one of our teens' family members back home in Omaha, and the emotional toll of another teen brought to tears when we heard the news of a shooting back in Omaha.

Still, our Jackson experience was highlighted with a tour and discussion with civil rights-era foot soldier Shirley Harrington, who experienced the brunt of racism in Mississippi firsthand and had worked with civil rights leader Evans, who was assassinated in his driveway in 1963.

The teens' focus sharpened. We broke the youth into teams with names of famous African Americans from our history for the study. This group of diverse youth began to bond. While working together on their nightly projects of journaling and reflecting, they began to transform. We went to bed in Montgomery, Alabama, and woke up on the third day, when we would visit Birmingham and Selma, the site of the infamous Edmund Pettus Bridge.

By the third and fourth days, we realized that not only were we were teaching African American history and culture — we were teaching character, responsibility, accountability, and interpersonal relationship skills.

Upon reflection, we also realized that the youth were watching us pray.

To begin each day, to begin each meal and to close the day, we prayed. Each day contained unique personal and transactional challenges that were met with prayer. We weren't teaching prayer; we just prayed. No specific doctrine or denomination, but prayer. One specific example comes to mind, when we had technical problems with our 12-passenger van. This was a major hurdle to the full participation of those traveling on the van. We prayed. And, unexpectedly, perhaps miraculously, the vendor sent a driver from Omaha to Montgomery with a replacement van.

They watched us pray.

By the end of our six-day tour, which concluded with tours in Tuskegee and Atlanta, we reflected and said, "Job well done." We had successfully impacted the character development of our youth, and we exposed and taught them their African American history. We taught the truth of the history of America and African Americans, including the horrible years of slavery, lynching, Jim Crowism, and 20th-century racism.

Let me address the disgusting debate about critical race theory. What we saw was truth.

My life experience and education refute any mention of theory to replace the facts of racism. And I submit as evidence the 2021 Black Votes Matter Tour, and I submit, and I pray, that this ridiculous assault on truth will lose its way, and the youth who attended the 2021 tour will give witness to the truth.

| AN ESSAY COLLECTION |

Redistricting in Nebraska

We mourn the tragedies of Covid-19 and its mutant Delta, wildfires, floods, hurricanes, tornados, death and destruction, and life-changing occurrences because of them. In addition to those nature-based tragedies, we mourn man's invasion into peace, harmony, and love, with complex racial and gender attacks, hate, political posturing, total dysfunction, and ultimately the attack on Democracy. We mourn, but we pray for our people and our country.

With all of these levels of hardships that we face, our personal challenge is to press on, continue with hope, advocacy and activism. We press on with an eye towards the future of our children and normalcy. We find ourselves challenged to stay focused amidst the surrounding trauma, the frontal attacks on our Democracy and our common sense. How did misinformation, big lies, hate and white supremacy get their footing? We must press on.

We must press on to save our planet from violent climate change, save the world from war and rumors of war, terrorism, save our country from infrastructure and moral decay, the dilution of the checks and balances in our three branches of government, and the undermining and suppression, of Democracy's basics—voting rights for everyone. We must press on.

In Nebraska, we come upon another responsibility, to translate our most recent 2020 Census Count and its resulting population shifting (mostly from rural to urban) and redraw the district boundaries for our State Senate legislative districts and our three Congressional Districts. What's at stake is who represents the people. This process is called redistricting. Redistricting has the potential for Nebraska to be the good, the bad, or the ugly.

For the record, redistricting attempts to make the various State Legislative Districts and the Congressional Districts relatively equal in population and provide a fair method and a fair resulting state and federal districts. That's the good.

The lines can be drawn to alter the balance of power in a way that is not representative of voters and undermines the equality and fairness of the one person, one vote rule, and to not preserve recognizable and cohesive communities. That's the bad.

The bad becomes the ugly when there is a manipulation of the district lines to give one political party an advantage over another. Often it allows parties and politicians in power to stay in power by creating an unfair advantage. That ugly process is called "gerrymandering."

Nebraska has started the process of redistricting. The Nebraska Legislature has been charged with managing and conducting the redistricting process. Drafts of initial maps are in progress, and a redistricting committee, made up of nine state senators, is in the process of reviewing and getting public input on those maps. By November, the legislature will approve and vote on final matters, and by December, the Governor will sign, or veto, the supporting legislation.

We, as a people, need to press on, participate, become watchdogs to ensure that the redistricting process does not become "bad" or "gerrymandering." We need to be in contact with our Senators, we need to be in contact with our Senators who are on the Redistricting Committee, we need to attend public hearings to make our voices heard, and we need to educate and spread the word to our fellow citizens.

Many organizations are providing information to the public and providing fair maps for consideration. I mention the League of Women Voters, and Common Cause, as an example. In our area, Senators Carol Blood from Bellevue, Steve Lathrop and Justin Wayne from Omaha are on the 2021 Nebraska Redistricting Committee.

There are redistricting hearings planned. The following dates and locations have been announced for the Redistricting Committee's public hearings on draft maps:

- September 15 at 9:00 am, Nebraska State Capitol Bldg., 1445 K St., Room 1524, Lincoln, NE
- September 16 at 10:00 am, Scott Conference Center, 6450 Pine St., Omaha, NE

Black Votes Matter Institute of Community Engagement will be conducting a Town Hall Meeting intended to educate the public on interacting, participating, and giving input to the redistricting process.

That Town Hall Meeting will take place on Tuesday, September 14, 2021, at 6:00 pm, at 2514 North 24th Street.

My recommendation to <u>decline to sign</u> the petition is being circulated in order to put on the next election ballot an initiative to change the constitution to require Voter ID before voting in Nebraska. We don't need Voter ID; we don't need to alter our constitution; we need only to press on.

| AN ESSAY COLLECTION |

2024: The Fall of the Empire?

The recent news of a potential Presidential run of Donald Trump for president in 2024 signifies the transition from the slow drip, drip leaking of Democracy to a fire-hose flow and the fall of our great empire.

As an adjunct Professor, the potential Trump candidacy coincides with recent dialogues I am having with my class at the University of Nebraska at Omaha on the impediments to voting faced by people of color and otherwise. Those intentional impediments or restrictions included literacy test, grandfather clauses, poll tax, violence and intimidations and the list go on. The combination of Trump's formal announcement, and the discussions with my diverse students, brings me to the awesome and shocking possibility that Democracy in America has lost its way. It should be noted that the discussion with the students was not about Trump's candidacy, far from it, but centered around why people of color's propensity to vote is waning. A couple of things need to be noted:

1. Any discussion of a waning vote in America may seem to be out of sync with the record number of nearly 150 million voters in the 2020 election. I contend that the record number of votes cast by Trump supporters saw the 2020 election as a last gasp to elect somebody (Trump) who promised to "make America great again" in 2016, but in reality, realized that the promise was for a return to times where Democracy was symbolic and not real to all. They liked the idea that Trump would get them there.
Contrarily, the vote for Biden was, in reality, a vote against returning to the days of bigotry, overt and unaccountable racism, white supremacy, voting restrictions and rampant disparities for people of color that Trump represented. It was a vote against Trump, as much as a vote for Biden. I contend that the record turnout in 2020 was statistically great, but mostly for all the wrong reasons on both sides.

2. No analysis of the 2020 election can make sense of why nearly over 70 million people chose to vote for a twice-impeached presidential incumbent, who activated white supremacy, activated attacks on women's rights, and on women in particular, with vulgar verbalizations, intentionally unplugged America with its global allies, climate change, covert relationships with Russia, a targeted attack on women's right to choose, corrupt and illegal financial dealings, record numbers of his administration forced to a flagrant disregard to the protocols of our intelligence community, disregard to the rule of law, laughable response to the COVID-19 crisis, and unbelievable as it may be, to lead and create an attempt to overthrow the works of our government on January 6, 2021. I submit this shortlist only to make my point. Please note that this discussion is about Trump. NOT about Democrats vs. Republicans.

In my book, *Economic Cataracts*, written in 2015, about my dismay, analysis, and perspective on the obstacles of urban community engagement and economic inclusion, that partly centered on why people of color historically vote at an alarming rate below that of our White counterparts. So, my recent discussion with my university class about the voting disparities of people of color uncovered the thoughts of my White, African, African American and Latino students. They are dismayed with the state of our Democracy and express it by saying that the political divisiveness is completely omitting issues that relate to their future. Climate change, women's rights, health care, big money. America's promises made and not kept, the lack of diversity, equity and inclusion, the lack of proper civic education, and the lack of attention to the survival of Democracy dominate their observations. They express confusion over why so many sign up and believe in the big lies being told constantly.

If Trump does run for president in 2024, there are two things that I conclude:

1. **If Trump wins**, we will return to his dismantling of America's Democracy. He will rule, not govern, and the divisive gap will be too wide for America to bridge. As we saw for four years of Trump, accountability and governmental checks and balances can be bullied and ignored.

2. **If Trump loses**, there will be the return of big lies, and Democracy will crumble, lacking the ability to conduct and complete an election. Destructive behavior, as you see now relating to the 2020 election and its associated divisiveness, will be beyond repair. In other words, the fall of our empire. November 2024. Win or lose, Trump will destroy the nation.

Note, there are some odds that Trump is faking a real announcement to run in 2024 in order to raise money to pay for his lifestyle and/or his legal problems. That's another story for another time. All Americans must fight for Democracy, not demagoguery.

---- AN ESSAY COLLECTION ----

Save Our Children

It has been a topic of my mental anguish for several years: the plight and the state of affairs of our young—our children and our youth. My mental gyrations have been based on no scientific data or empirical evidence to prove what I thought I saw before me, which was a metamorphosis in our young people. Our youth have been bombarded with a series of disconnected events that have contributed to a new generation and a new composite of our youth, both youth of color and white youth. I respectfully submit to this mental process, a list of those contributory factors:

- The emergence of a generational virus (Covid 19) threatening the life of family, friends, and even oneself.
- The observation of extreme divisionalization and disconnect, rooted in race, gender, economic status, political affiliations, generations. Please note it could be a combination of any or all of the items listed.

- Extreme divisiveness is rooted in hate or supremacy, and is interconnected with all of those various divisions we have.
- The uncertainty of career opportunities (not jobs, but careers), and the seeming disconnect between their educational sacrifices, to a life of financial and personal security.
- The realities of inequity, lack of diversity, and the lack of inclusion, will dominate their adult lives.
- Their unfortunate realization, by observations, is that big lies and misinformation go unchecked and are supported by such a large segment of our community. In other words, the fleeting fabric of truth.
- Their observations that the adults are troubled with being accountable for the future. For example, what are the adults doing to guarantee a world not ruined by climate change, toxic water, and more?

Repeating myself, our youth are highly affected by the facts and observations. They are changed and are inclined to have mental health challenges because of this drama and uncertainty. And, most of their challenges are not readily obvious to us as adults.

May I teach from the point of wisdom? Youth of color have another layer to reckon with, and it's mostly rooted in multi-generational poverty. Multi-generational poverty generates a sub-culture of inferiority, desperation, anger, community disconnect and lawlessness. An example, crime and the drug trade. Drug trade generates more crime, violence, murder, and more because the drug trade generates a unique opportunity for cash flow in a poverty-stricken community. I implore readers not to judge the victims but judge the circumstances. Above all, understand the root and the cause of many of the problems within our urban centers. In the news, I recently read about violence, fights, and disruptions in our schools and realized that they are rooted in generational poverty.

I submit to you two recent pieces of evidence to make my point that our youth have changed:

3. My recent southern Black History Tour, where I take 40 high school kids on an annual Civil Rights history journey throughout the South. For five years, we have traveled with over 250 youth, but in 2021, the youth we traveled with were different. The evidence of all of the factors mentioned above had impacted this year's group. They were significantly harder to manage, discipline, and get them to focus and develop them as to learning, caring, and leadership. We made an impact, but it was much harder. They were different.

4. In my university class at UNO, we discuss items from my book, *Economic Cataracts*, written in 2015, regarding obstacles of urban community engagement and reduced voting enthusiasm. My surprise, from former class discussions, is that this year's class seemed to refocus the normal discussion into a discussion of not the realities of urban communities, but the discussion of their own communities, and the lack of political and society's commitment to their future, such as was mentioned, climate change, equity, women's rights, environment and more. My detection is that they expressed confusion and uncertainty about the state of affairs and the future of Democracy.

My confession is that I share the same concerns, the same uncertainties. I have the advantage of living most of my life already, and the waters have flowed under my bridge, but our youth are just going to the river for a drink and have a thirst for a full life. They are begging for the recognition of the adults to understand that their future is in our hands. I agree. We need to save our children. I challenge us all to lay down our divisiveness and focus on doing whatever is necessary to save our children, not just sit back and see what happens.

---AN ESSAY COLLECTION---

North Omaha Begins a New Chapter

July 4 of this year, I turn 80 years old. I have lived, witnessed, experienced, and even studied the evolution of my beloved North Omaha, for all of my years. I have studied the fact that we have had two lynchings in Omaha, we've experienced the devastating effects of racism, discriminatory practices, redlining, segregated schools, and lack of access to public and private accommodations because of race, the killing of 14-year-old Vivian Strong by police in 1969, and much more.

Yet despite that, I've witnessed the glory of North Omaha, and its wonderful history, heritage and culture. We have produced some of the greatest people in America, in every aspect of life: athletics, (God Bless our beloved late Marlin Briscoe), professions, the arts, music, and in business, all of which are too numerous to mention, but worthy to be noted in the aggregate.

In the past, North Omaha was vibrant in every way: in church, in commerce and community. While we were a poverty-stricken community, we were rich in our culture and in our social fiber and family. When discriminated against, in most areas within our community, we produced our own alternatives. Two examples: when white mortuaries refused to bury Blacks, we created generationally successful mortuaries of our own, and when the daily newspaper produced only bad and biased news about African Americans in North Omaha, we created our own, evidenced by the long-standing, Black newspaper, known as the *Omaha Star*.

The focus of this article is the historical economic devastation that this community has experienced for generations, and surely in my lifetime. My generation, in large percentages, left Nebraska as soon as we were mature enough or we had completed our high school or college educations. We left Nebraska to seek opportunities that were not available to us in our hometown. I could be counted in that number. But when we left, we drained our beloved North Omaha of our valuable brain power, our financial potential, our talents and skills; the community was destroyed repeatedly, in response to the many reactions we experienced from the killings of Vivian Strong, to the tumultuous times in the '60s, and more. These destructive events devastated our community and its vibrancy; the north freeway cut a slice through North Omaha and causes irreparable damage to our culture and economics. The resulting accumulation of these facts left North Omaha economically devastated. Evidence of that devastation that can still be seen in North Omaha.

I provide a service called the North Omaha Legacy Tours, where I guide a tour through our key corridors and teach about our culture and history, and part of that education involves the residual, and currently present, remains from years of economic devastation. That story is made more horrible by the fact that, in spite of all of the wonderful people and history and culture, there have been 40-50 years of economic neglect and disinvestment.

I submit to you that today North Omaha is turning the pages of history and beginning a new chapter. That chapter promises the long-awaited, thoughtful, and substantial, albeit not yet comprehensive, development of North Omaha. I submit the evidence of this new chapter: 10

wonderful, small to large, economic development projects, which are at different stages, but begin the new chapter of development in North Omaha.

1. The total renovation of the northwest corner sector of 24th and Lake, where the organization *Fabric* has totally renovated and upgraded the buildings on the northwest corner sector, from Lake Street to Ohio Street and a new music and arts venue called North Omaha Music and Arts (NOMA).
2. The Union for Contemporary Arts, which provides wonderful programming related to the arts and more, on the southeast corner of 24th and Lake.
3. On the southwest corner of 24th and Lake is the new and exciting Revive Center, which includes a place for meetings, lunches and events.
4. On the northeast corner of 24th and Lake is the exciting and dramatic plan for a $40 million dollar multi-use complex, built by African-American businesswoman Carmen Tapio's Forever North Development.
5. The planned, new Black Box Theater Complex, to be named after Shirley Tyree, being built by the Union for Contemporary Arts, which will provide a new live theater on North 24th Street.

6. The newly established financial institution in the historic Carver Savings and Loans building space, which will provide a new community-owned financial institution, located half a block off 24th Street. It comes from a partnership of the Willie and Yolanda Barney, Martin and Lynnell Williams and American National Bank.
7. The Small Business Complex, developed by the Omaha Economic Development Corporation, which includes small spaces for businesses, a restaurant, and more, in the newly developed Fair Deal Village at 24th and Burdette.
8. The potential new and wonderful development by an unannounced developer. in the Omaha OIC building, which has sat empty for nearly 20 years, and is now promised to provide a new and exciting venue.
9. Three significant renovations that include both the completed renovation of the old Carnation Ballroom at 24th and Miami, and to be completed, the renovation of the historical Spencer Street Barber Shop at 24th and Spencer, and the new and exciting CULXR House at 24th off Wirt.

10. Notwithstanding great new developments that are off the 24th Street corridor, but worth mentioning, are the potential of the expansion and visionary implementation of the Malcolm X Foundation at 34th and Evans, the exciting and responsible boxing gym, developed by Bud Crawford at Sprague and John Creighton Boulevard, the potential new development of the Ernie Chambers Museum on 20th and Ames Streets, and the North Omaha Trail which is currently under construction.

We celebrate all of the segments of a wonderful subchapter led by Carmen Tapio's Development. Together they represent wonderful new components that make up what is becoming North Omaha's new and exciting chapter of development. There are still many needs unaddressed. Hopefully our progress will be joined by recognition and respect of the greater community to provide comprehensive, but thoughtful major investment as partners and collaborators in this new chapter.

YOUR BRIDGE TO HISTORY
BY PORTIA LOVE & PRESTON LOVE JR.

Lothrop Elementary Book Reading, Feb. 2020

Girls Inc. Book Reading, Feb. 2020

Recommended for Grades 3-6
Bilingual (English & Spanish) edition available!
Contact: PrestonLoveJr@gmail.com or (402) 812-3324

2019 BVM Tour Group, Equal Justice Initiative, Montgomery, Alabama, June 2020

2019 BLACK VOTES MATTER "FACE-TO-FACE WITH BLACK HISTORY" TOUR

The Tour Destinations, 2020 & Beyond

Edmund Pettus Bridge, Selma, Alabama, June 2019

From Husker and Professional football player to IBM executive, now Civil Rights Historian and Racial Equity Advocate, Preston Love Jr. speaks with Congressman Jim Clyburn.

Honoring the legacy of his Dad and brothers

Youth leadership development seminar for high schools.

Frost becomes latest NU coach with COVID, says symptoms are mild. **Sports, Page B2**

Omaha World-Herald

MONDAY, JANUARY 10, 2022 • SUNRISE EDITION • REAL. FAIR. ACCURATE. OMAHA.COM

MILITARY VACCINE RULE
Defiance of order is sign of pandemic's politicization

Some active-duty forces refuse to be vaccinated, though more than 97% have had COVID shot

MELISSA HERNANDEZ
Los Angeles Times

Nickaylah Sampson seemed well on her way to achieving her dream of becoming an officer in the U.S. Army.

A stellar student whose family has a long tradition of military service, the San Antonio, Texas, native earned a coveted spot at West Point Military Academy.

She completed her freshman year in spring 2021, just as the military launched its vaccination campaign against COVID-19. Though she had no problem with the nine other vaccines the U.S. military requires upon enlistment, she said she worried that the COVID-19 shots were too new for their risks to be fully understood.

She said her parents, both Army veterans, told her that she had only one option: "Get out as quickly as you can."

So in October, Sampson, 19, quit West Point.

The latest data from the military shows that roughly 96,000 active-duty service members remain unvaccinated against COVID-19, despite a Defense Department mandate issued in August and deadlines that have passed.

Their defiance of a military order is a striking illustration of how deeply politicized the pandemic has become.

"Racism, sexism, addiction to compliance theories — you name it. If you can find it in the civilian population, you can find it within the military," said Peter Feaver, a

The Jewell Building near 24th and Grant Streets. The former Dreamland Ballroom now houses the Great Plains Black History Museum and the Omaha Economic Development Corporation. CHRIS MACHIAN, THE WORLD-HERALD

Tours with Love showcase his 'beloved community'

He shares 'rich history' of North Omaha

MARJIE DUCEY
World-Herald staff writer

When Preston Love Jr. talks about the history of the Jewell Building, near 24th and Grant Streets in North Omaha, he travels beyond the stories it's down in the famous Dreamland Ballroom.

Tales of how every famous African American musician once played there, from Count Basie to Duke Ellington, are just one aspect of the building, which now houses the Great Plains Black

WANT TO TAKE A TOUR?
If you want to schedule a tour, contact Preston Love Jr. at 402-812-3324 or preston@durban.org.

tours of the area to a new level. He's formed North Omaha Legacy Tours, he said, to inform people of the area's rich heritage and to stimulate growth on 24th and 30th Streets, the main arteries the tour follows.

The founder and director of the Institute for Urban Development says the tour will be known about

Tours

FROM A1

said, "Demystify and learn about North Omaha in a way they haven't done in the past."

It was unique that an African American named Jimmy Jewell had the wherewithal to finance a building such as the Jewell in the 1920s, Love said. He shares stories about the Omaha Star newspaper office across the street and the nearby Bryant Center, where many of the city's most famous athletes got their start.

Love then takes a more personal dive into the Jewell's history, recounting how his father, Preston Love Sr., as a young man would hide on the fire escape to listen to the musical greats who visited.

One night, he was caught by Basie, a jazz pianist who never forgot the youngster who could play the saxophone with such skill. He eventually hired him to fill in when his band was short, the first step on Love' Sr.'s own lifetime musical career.

Those stories help you understand the culture and significance behind the structures of note in his North Omaha neighborhood, Love said.

"If you really want a tour, you need all of that in context with the culture and history," he said.

That's why Kathy Ingoby Moore and several others from Presbyterian Church of the Cross in west Omaha recently took a morning tour with Love. It was part of an initiative they've started, Agape for All, in which they are learning about diverse parts of the Omaha community.

"This is going to be such a good learning opportunity for people," she said. "Many people don't really know the history of North Omaha."

Her favorite parts of the tour were stops at the Malcolm X Memorial Foundation and the Revive Center Omaha for lunch.

Willie Barney, CEO and founder of The Empowerment Network and co-founder of the Revive Center with his wife, Yolanda, spoke at the Revive Center and was amazing, she said, connecting the history shared by Love to future development in the area.

Barney said he and his wife have worked for years to emphasize the arts, culture and business opportunities available in North Omaha. He said Love's tours will help accelerate that effort.

"Many visitors from out of town and even a local residents in the city of Omaha don't know the rich history, the amazing culture or the business and entertainment options available for the whole family here at 24th and Lake and

A corner of 24th and Lake Streets in January 1968. Preston Love Jr. calls it "ground zero," the iconic center of North Omaha. "It always has been and presently still is. As I see what is happening in the future it will continue to be."

The Malcolm X Memorial Foundation is one of the stops on the tour.

Love brings a unique touch to the stories that illustrate North Omaha's history with North Omaha Legacy Tours.

throughout North Omaha," Barney said. "The tour gives them a chance to experience the great things happening in North Omaha firsthand."

Love said his favorite part of a tour is when people can

"I didn't know that." He'll hear it when he shares a story about Malcolm X's life in Omaha or that Ellington played here.

"That's the quote I hear constantly," he said. "We have a rich story to tell."

About 40 people from Moore's church were on the tour that she took recently. Love charges $30 fee an hour tour or $45 for two hours. Lunch or coffee of some books that detail the area's history can add another $15 to the cost and bring funds to the area.

Love is excited that comes here for the Coffee

World Series or the Berkshire Hathaway meetings or just people from other neighborhoods might want to take some time to learn about where he grew up. That will have an economic impact, help the area proudly move forward and bridge cultural gaps, he said.

"It's my beloved community," he said, "and the more I can teach people about our wonderful history the better."

marjie.ducey@owh.com, 402-444-1034, twitter.com/mduceyowh

April 16 at 4:01 PM

Today I took my kids on the North Omaha Legacy Bus Tour with our guide Preston Love Jr.

This tour was courtesy of the Urban Youth B.O.L.T. program with the Center For Holistic Development, Inc., where I also work as the Program Manager for the Family Support and GrandFriends African American adult mentoring programs.

Doris Moore Michelle Butler Preston Love Jr

4Urban.org
February 17

"Her favorite parts of the tour were stops at the Malcolm X Memorial Foundation and the Revive Center Omaha for lunch."

Contact Preston Love Jr to reserve your seat today!

https://omaha.com/.../article_e434e92e-6d9b-11ec-9a60...

OMAHA.COM
Tours with Preston Love Jr. share 'rich history' of North Omaha

An Octogenarian's Insights

Insight to Action

Preston Love Jr.'s creation of the Institute for Urban Development— More Simply, 4Urban.org

Preston Love, Jr., understands that thought—at least the best insights—deserve and must become community action at both the local and national levels! As a civil rights activist, professor of Black Studies, economic development expert, youth leadership development instructor, historian, and tour guide, Preston desires to formalize his approach across a local tour, regional Diversity, Equity, and Inclusion training & consulting, and the national BVM Tour for youth and adults. As Executive Director of Black Votes Matter Institute of Community Engagement since 2017, Preston chose to expand the mission and reach of his institute by branding his work with the registered trade name, **Institute for Urban Development, or 4Urban.org.**

4Urban.org's mission is to become a thought-leader in developing urban communities through community engagement, economic growth initiatives, leadership growth opportunities, and Get Out The

Vote initiatives. 4Urban informs, educates, and acts to raise the quality of life for all with emphasis in the economically disadvantaged, diverse, and multi-ethnic populations.

The Institute's 4 Pillars

Community Engagement
Economic Growth
Leadership Growth
Black Votes Matter (Get Out the Vote)

Community Engagement

- Experienced Community Organizer
- Facilitator & Lecturer
- Champion of Innovative Engagement Strategies

Economic Growth

- Diversity, Equity & Inclusion Training & Consulting for Growth
- Keynote Speaking
- Award-Winning, National Author

Leadership Growth

- Face-to-Face with Black History Youth & Adult Tours along the Civil Rights Trail
- North Omaha Legacy Tours
- Children's Books
- Consulting in Youth Leadership Development

Black Votes Matter (Get Out the Vote)

- Community Organizing Expertise
- Nonpartisan Insights
- Campaign Consulting

NORTH OMAHA LEGACY TOUR

With an identified need to increase cultural & historical understanding of North Omaha while increasing tourism and economic growth for North Omaha, 4Urban conducts a first-class, professional tour for the benefit of visitors, small businesses, and the Omaha Metro.

4Urban.org is a registered trade name of Black Votes Matter Institute

The objectives of the North Omaha Legacy Tour are

- To demystify North Omaha's reputation to greater understanding creating pathways to collaboration

- To inform participants of North Omaha's rich heritage, legacy, and historical contributions
- Stimulate economic growth along North Omaha's key corridors
- To instill pride for North Omaha

From North 24th St. to the 30th St. corridor, and the Malcolm X Foundation, celebrate the past and embrace the future with us on this wonderful, entertaining tour of North Omaha. North 24th St., known as "The Street of Dreams" and affectionately named "The Deuce," has hosted some of the greats in American Jazz history and is still a home for the arts. Our expert host is eager to share stories of the rich legacy of this area and the African-American community, including the stories of Malcolm Little, later known as Malcolm X. Hear authentic local stories about why North Omaha is a beacon of the past and important for the future.

Our Collaborative Partners Include:

- Great Plains Black History Museum & Dreamland Ballroom
- North End Teleservices LLC
- Fair Deal Market
- *The Omaha Star*
- The Union for Contemporary Art
- Revive! Omaha
- Broomfield Rowhouse
- Terence "Bud" Crawford Gym & TBC Shop
- SPARK / Black Votes Matter Institute
- Carnation Ballroom
- CULXR House
- The Highlander & Big Mama's restaurant
- Salem Baptist Church
- Urban League of Nebraska
- Malcolm X Memorial Foundation
- Historical Black Churches

DIVERSITY, EQUITY, & INCLUSION TRAINING & CONSULTING

To understand where to begin with **Diversity, Equity, and Inclusion (DEI) training**, one must measure the current state of DEI issues as they reside in an organization's culture. Otherwise, consultants randomly throw darts at the DEI topic dartboard to decide the next organizational training objective. 4Urban.org offers a *unique approach* to understanding an organization's culture to uncover and prioritize the DEI topics essential to moving the organization to a better place. Unfortunately, training for the sake of training is a last-century approach. Instead, 4Urban.org employs a proven and proprietary approach to identifying the *most needed* DEI topics in a timely and effective way and then delivers those topics through world-class training conducted by Preston Love, Jr. an experienced academic, businessman, nonprofit leader, and civil rights activist.

Our methodology uses a qualitative and quantitative sensemaking platform to capture the numerous stories of a given population, from employees and management alike. Study results enable the organization to holistically understand its current culture, the efficacy of programs and initiatives, and chart a course towards its desired end state. The stories collected represent real people and their sentiment towards their experiences with an organization. They are *data with a soul*.

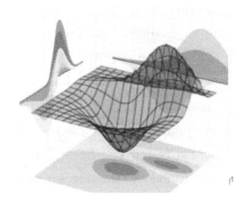

4Urban.org recently completed a study with a prominent University on Diversity, Equity, & Inclusions (DEI) issues within that University's Athletic Department and its 400 student-athletes. The results were surprising to all involved, from the Athletic Director to Sports Team Coaches. As a result, we are expressly interested in what your results will bring to your leadership team.

4Urban.org has partnered with CFOUR Foundation, a data science company, and Spryng.io, the sensemaking software platform to offer a holistic capture of the sentiment towards an organization and the effectiveness of its programs/initiatives over time. The distributed narrative collection and quantitative data analysis enable decision-makers to understand their environment or complex challenges from the tactical to operational and strategic levels.

4Urban DEI study objectives begin with and are customized to client needs and include:

- Collecting and signifying narrative stories of the client organization's DEI perspectives.
- Reducing the cognitive bias in the client organizations through conversations and experiences
- Identifying the emerging trends and risks associated with moving forward

For more information, check out our "Breaking the Bubble" Overview video!

https://bit.ly/4urbanBubble

BVM "Face-to-Face With Black History" Youth & Adult Tour

The seed for the Black Votes Matter Youth initiative is as a response to the lack of knowledge of Black history and the civil rights movement. In order for our youth to become effective leaders, they must learn and have respect for their own history. The Black Votes Matter Tour was designed to address this void.

Through Memphis, Jackson, Birmingham, Selma, Montgomery, Tuskegee, and Atlanta, our tour averages 60 total participants with 40 of those being high school students, mostly from Omaha Public Schools. We have trained cadre staff, a registered nurse, and chaperones. Our participants experience the venue and our youth programming includes mobile microlearning, daily reflections, and journaling. The participants experience non-violent methods of the '60s, such as the lunch counter sit-in protest in Atlanta's National Center for Civil and Human Rights museum. The youth and adults are prepared to respond to today's challenges through small group discussions, practical applications, and continued journaling. They become confident in discussing human rights and advocating for economic empowerment through the Black Votes Matter Institute.

Check out our 2021 highlight tour video: https://youtu.be/QewmOsmU_iE

GENERAL WORKSHOPS, SPEAKING EVENTS

AUDIENCE SPECIFIC

Executives, management, employees, small groups, and individuals

VARIETY OF TOPICS

- Assuming a lens of anti-racism and racial equity in daily operations
- DEI organizational values, team development, unconscious bias/implicit bias, fragility, privilege

INTENDED TO PROVIDE INSIGHTS AND SENSITIVITY

- Hard-hitting, memorable, and a unique insight to racial equity success
- Ongoing assessment demonstrating effectiveness in diversity, equity, and inclusion programs, and the efficacy in specific initiatives

CONTACT

Preston Love, Jr., Executive Director, 4Urban.org

6021 Villa De Santa Dr.

Omaha, NE 68104

Email: preston@4urban.org

www.4urban.org

4Urban.org is a registered trade name of Black Votes Matter Institute of Community Engagement, a 501(c)(3) nonprofit organization. Tax deductible donations will further the mission of 4Urban.org and may be sent to the mailing address above or contact Preston via email to donate on PayPal.

Made in the USA
Monee, IL
30 September 2022

14968236R00085